Amy Tollyfield

The Suicide

Olympia Publishers
London

www.olympiapublishers.com
OLYMPIA PAPERBACK EDITION

A CIP catalogue record for this title is
available from the British Library.

ISBN: 978-1-78830-206-7

First Published in 2018

Olympia Publishers
60 Cannon Street
London
EC4N 6NP

Printed in Great Britain

About the Author

Amy Tollyfield has studied MA Shakespeare Studies and BA (Hons) Drama and Theatre Practice, but her favourite study remains to be the female allure. Amy has always believed in God and enjoys analysing the human condition. Her writing, like her soul, wants to obtain something deeper. May you find it here.

The Suicide

Dedication

To Nanny

Acknowledgments

I'd like to thank my parents and friends for reading my work, and God, who has always strengthened me and provided for me.

The Suicide

You fasten the harness. It's bigger than you,
But that isn't hard when you're five fucking two.
Ever the righteous, prim renegade,
The floor has been hoovered, the bed has been made.

The photo of your family is now oddly soothing,
(Even if it's queer that Mum's eyes are moving),
And you really wish that you had touched up the paint
Given more time. Hasty slapdash you ain't.

There are scratch-marks on the wall; you don't know
where from.
No girl has been here since time has begun!
However, maybe, these lines tell a story:
'Twenty-four-year-old woman clings to former glory,

'And desperately scratches her name in the wall,
'Recording her errors, documenting her fall!'
Yes, yes, that shit will make the news,
(Along with your conflicting hard right-wing views).

You think you'll miss nobody, least of all the cat.
You still have a mark on the floor where he shat,
And all of your family you secretly despise
(Especially Mum, and her weird, roving eyes).

You could have been something, you could have made
dollar,
Riding in a Benz, leaning out, shouting 'holla!'
Your ex-girlfriend appears, slaps you in the face!
Yes, yes, that's good. We're gaining some pace.

As if you'd do all of this and not wash the sheets!
Lining up all your copies of Shelley and Keats,
And countless other books that you never read.
(You've gotta look interesting when they come find you
dead.)

You're happiest in the bath, reading *Heat!* or *Kerrang*,
Or sipping a coffee, not giving a damn!
For all of the lost time, the wasted potential,
You turn to the noose, whisper, 'sweetheart, be gentle.'

Doorways

I pray through doorways,
Hiding out
In the middle of the ocean,
Drifting into
Purple golds.

You will never know,
And I will draw every short straw
Until I wake to evergreen,
In a bed which is empty.

On your wedding day,
I shall not be seen,
I will be the not -
It does not matter -
And you will begin.

On your deathbed,
I will be lonely.
Remember me
And what might have been.

Pomegranate Stars

I have danced under pomegranate stars
And I remembered the elixir that carried you home.
The faint memories were nought but hours
And the time spent with you was never alone.

I dropped into a minor chord for all my trouble.
They waited the clock on subsequent endings.
I tasted time like a pop from a bubble,
With dewdrops and honey my only befriendings.

I sit a while and pray in the pew of a church.
This is my solace and I am now complete.
My God is the one who remembers my search
And the tap-tap-tap of my pomegranate feet.

Marrow

Her bones became marrow on the inside of the wall,
I could hear her heart racing as her eyes covered in snow.
I watched the events unfold without drinking it all,
And I slumped into my chair as I tried to let it go.

The days became a whisper in the interim that followed.
I did not see her, call her, or even cross her path.
It was not to be the case that either of us wallowed,
It was simply that we lived in two separate parts of Bath.

On the seventh day I decided that I would be the one
To invite her out for dinner and to take her for a drink.
Later we would find that we wanted to be fun,
And to be the happy couple washing dishes by the sink.

Graves

I have stood among graves
And felt such peace,
Like someone is watching me
Such tender release:
To feel their bones crack
Deep down underneath
And to know that I am them
And that one day my lease
Will fully expire
And I'll be the beast
Who favours the ground
To any earthly retreats.
So one day I'll hide
Deep down in the throes
And you can wait for me there
Where every man goes.

Daffodils

Churchyard.
Cold,
Silent
Breeze.

Imagine
Your footsteps are like
The day I rose again
Among the daffodils.

Cleaning Windows

Among the dust we found only ourselves,
Once the debris had settled.
Our oxygen masks removed,
We awoke to tender air.

I watched daybreak with the same remorse.
I was cold, challenged, aware, with
My irises illuminated to pitch black
And my hair a radiant sapphire.

There is no awakening amongst lengthy stays.
The twilight beckons into watchful hours.
I trace the outline of my cup,
And watch the tap drip in sorrows.

I am now a beacon of the truth.
My oranges become silver like the moon.
The patience of my virtue lets you go,
And you return, return, return.

One Day

One day,
When I am much older,
And when I can support myself financially,
I will hop on a plane
And fly to New York.

No one will know where I have gone,
Because I won't have told them.

And when I am there,
I will rent out an apartment
Several storeys high
So that I can see
All of New York.

Still no one will know where I have gone,
Because I won't have told them.

And I will work in an office
And read emails

And drink coffee
And dress smartly
And read Vogue.

People will no longer care where I have gone,
Because I never told them.

And one day,
When I go for my choca-mocha-latte,
I will bump into you
And you will come back to mine
And we will live together.

And you will know where I have gone
Because I have told you.

Baxter and Sunrise

I remember sitting with the moon
And watching as it tried to make sense to me.
A man approaches, noticing my lame dog.
He offers us a fifty pence piece
But I am not interested.

Earnestly, I cling to the backs of dirty buildings,
Smog and firepit filling my lungs.
Baxter's eyes glint golden at the crack of dawn,
And he yawns into the day.

When the cigarette butts pile high,
Baxter nuzzles close against my thigh
And we rise together, the most earnest of contemporary
politicians,
Stumbling to a new life
On the other side of the city
Where we will laugh, pray, mock, guffaw
And catch hope in our solitude.

Narcotics

I remember the first hit.
It was like energy in my lungs
And you were there
And you told me to sit down.

I remember the doctor's note,
The scratches up my arm,
The pale, incandescent weeping,
The bright lights,
The physiotherapist,
The infernal schoolboy outside
Banging his football against the glass,
Chiming in rhythm with my headaches.

Each score cost me more;
Rent, bus fare, dentist bills.
We were broken, gone, destitute,
And I looked to you like a shadow.

My eyes squint against the sallow stream of light
To catch the moment when,
Against all odds,
And witnessing the scar tissue,
You hold my hand tighter than a rock
To risk this perilous path.

Innermost

I am a dog in the innermost shadow.
You do not hear me pine for you.
I touch the wall we embellished on
And let the stars align for you.

Please wake into a blissful slumber.
I shall not disturb you or your rest.
I shall be the voice which never utters,
And dream of sleeping upon your breast.

Do not fill up my food bowl.
The crumbs you left will feed me tonight.
I scratch at bedposts wistfully;
I know that tomorrow will bring daylight.

You are the beginning of a happy time.
Please dry your eyes and know your heart.
I am a dog in the innermost shadow
And I long for you to have a new start.

Graffiti

Passing colour, you cock your head:
A vision in magenta, in purple, in red.
The pain of sinner, but rarely a saint
Is here for you, tenderly written in paint.

The life of a paintbrush, the death of a scrawl
Is thrown into nature, and falls to the wall.
Those that pass, for a moment or two
Connect with the lifeless: those forgotten, small few.

If statues could move, if these walls could speak,
They'd champion the homeless, the modest, the weak,
So all could see, that when it comes to man,
Every creature has a home in God's plan.

Sometimes

Sometimes,
Out of the darkest storm,
Dreams whisper
From the shadows, take form;
Linger just briefly
Upon the ears of kings
And settle as dust
On the eagle's wings.

She takes her flight,
Wandering foreign lands.
Her agility protects her
From foreign hands.
She swoops to the mountains,
And low to the coast.
That small piece of dust
Still pea-size (at most).

She witnesses battles,
The burning of homes,

The cyber invasions,
The releasing of drones.
She wanders and cries -
No eggs of her own -
And watches and listens
Her keens into moans.

Her pain is apparent.
She's no longer afraid.
Evading capture
Becomes no longer her trade.
She settles in danger.
She lets them begin.
They take her to chains,
And she's kept, and they win.

Months become years.
Her feathers receding,
She stifles alone,
Too wounded for bleeding.
Food loses its taste.
Wine tastes as water.
Hell took the lion
As lamb to the slaughter.

As day turns to night
Once again in these caves,
The setting sun illuminates
One of her blades.

She blinks back her apathy -
Glimpses at first -
Then stares with a hunger
At her own wings. The thirst!

Water is wine!
Her dreams do unfold.
The speck of dust shows her
That she yet may find gold.
She shakes off her shackles
(Which in truth, were not there),
And flies in the moonlight
To the only place where-

Sometimes,
Out of the darkest storm,
Dreams whisper
From the shadows, take form;
Linger just briefly,
And then become true.
The eagle may wander
But she will come to find you.

Dear Friend

Dear friend, I write to you from this lonely shore,
Though yours is a face I don't see anymore.
I untied my hands by melting the wax:
Burning the candle until I knew all the facts.

My soul is alive, and no longer impeached.
I no longer feel guilty for all that you teached.
I hope that you dance near our basket of wicker,
Troubled as you are. Watch my flame go a-flicker.

Let me once more take your hand in the night
And guide you to safety. Purge the moonlight!
You know not to trust the steel in my gaze.
I live only for me. My basket is ablaze.

Throw it out, my precious wicket basket!
Find the hole that still lives in this empty casket.
Burn, burn, burn. Bright and intense.
Think of me still when you light your incense.

Beneath The Plane

Cityscape
Soft as your nape,
Blurry as gas,
Below does pass.

LEDs
Soft as the seas
Glow in the dusk,
Illuminating rust.

Cobbled lanes,
The tracks of trains,
Scatter and patter
As gentle as rain.

Another town,
Another name,
Passes beneath,
Beneath the plane.

Ask

Dawn is as dusk
In this lowly land.
The heathen bush shakes.
The earth is tanned.

The sun never sets.
The dogs only growl.
No rooftops are glistening.
No call of the owl.

The quiet is deafening,
As is the air.
No eyes will meet yours
And yet something will stare.

Sinister as it is,
If you can survive,
Dear prizes await you
On the other side.

Dealing

My dear,
Do not mix
Dealing with feeling.
One does the hurt,
And the other the healing.

Take a back step
From your
Aces and spades.
None of those diamonds,
And not the old maids.

Do not roll the dice
On yesterday's
Gains.
One fills your pocket,
The other your pains.

Blackjack is calling
And Russian

Roulette.
But if you dare not to answer,
There's gold for you yet.

Clarence

These were uncertain times, and it was amiss to dismiss
The plottings of a brother as innocent and harmless,
So Edward can be forgiven for choosing to put
His brother in wine; drowned in a Malmsey butt.

George was a fool! He ranted and raved.
His language was slanderous, unforgiving, depraved.
He sided with evil and lended his name
To giving his lecherous brother the shame-

Of being thought illegitimate. George turned up with
priests
At Edward's banquet (the most illustrious of feasts!),
And read from a scroll Edward's alleged misdoings,
All of them false, sealing only his own undoing.

George was sentenced to death for his traitorous crime,
And met his end in a vat of his favourite wine.
The Tower walls are happy to witness him drown.
Do not set your sights on your own brother's crown.

Unsorry

There are no flaws so intense as mine
And in the night-time they do not fail to shine.
You pick up my wings and sprinkle them with dust,
But the wings harden, then decay, then rust.

The morning sun illuminates all of my folly,
For which I am - truly - never really sorry,
And between the hyacinths that glitter below,
I pray for the sunlight to fall only as snow.

Your patience abounds. You save me through grace
And as I cry, I notice only your face,
And through these tender cracks of right and wrong,
You help me find a way to write my own song.

Rosé

She gave me a smile on that midsummer evening,
The kind that reminds you that you are still breathing.
Your heart does a somersault, reaches the ceiling,
Dances and flips, and keeps you believing.

She bumped me with hips many-a-time,
Intoxicated with lust and sweet rosé wine.
She fluttered those lashes and came back to mine,
And met me in bed, where we met the sublime.

She moved to a city. I've no idea where.
I'd love to know, but then I also don't care,
Because hers was a body which she liked to share
And all of my jealousy got me nowhere.

If you're reading this, and you're feeling quite lonely,
Reminiscing a time when you were her only,
Remember that taste is far from the truth,
And we gain in our age what we lacked in our youth.

Pentecost

When they come for you
(And they will come for you),
I'll be the first to hold them back.
My blood-soaked eyes,
(My only disguise),
Will be hiding these lies
From your crimson red skies.

Let me bask in this illusion for five minutes more.
Hold the Pentecost back against the timber-framed door.
I'll still cook the dinner, lay this table for four
And dress all in pink. I'll wipe the stains from the floor.

I didn't know you were capable
(But it's good to have closure).
Let your monster run free with all its ugly exposure.
I'll still be your family -
Burning your candle -
Lighting the spark
That makes you fly off the handle.

When it burns out
And the wax comes anew,
You'll be in your cell and your friends will be few.
Your visiting times
For your long list of crimes
Will be filled up with me.
Wash my eyes,
Me and you.

Dear Future Ex-Wife

'Dear future ex-wife...'
Wow, that really has a ring!
Not like the one I bought you.
Apparently that didn't mean a thing!

I'm sorry I was jealous.
It's just, you really did the rounds.
Next time he comes over
Could you make sure he pays in pounds?

We had some good times overall,
Like the time we went to Rome.
In fact, we had so much fun
That you weren't on the plane home.

Thank you for the memories,
And for raising our two boys.
The youngest one is just like you-
An annoying ball of noise.

You really had a thing for teeth,
But then you were an orthodontist.
You kept bags of molars in the living room
Between Star Trek and Pocahontas.

I do look back and smile
But I shall not miss your snores.
In fact your night-time mumblings
Were the few words I didn't ignore.

I wish you all the very best
In life and love and stuff.
I hope that all your future lovers
Are not quite good enough.

But most of all, I wish that you
Would please return my ring.
My heart it bleeds, the day you left-
I paid a fortune for that thing.

Big Sea

I was sixteen.
Don't even ask me
What life was like at sixteen
Because I categorically,
Systematically
Do not want to talk about it.

She was switched on.
Hardwired to ask
All of the right questions.
She told me that I could be
A big fish in a small pond
If I stayed at their sixth form.

I was sixteen
But very, very sharp.
I wanted to go somewhere bigger,
Somewhere with a bit of a buzz,
Maybe even be
A small fish in a large sea.

I'm twenty-five.
I still have the itch.
In my carriage
Are other small fish -
Swimming, swimming -
In love with the big sea.

Dice

I roll the dice
In every corner.
It waxes and it wanes
As I watch you.

Don't go to sleep.
I can hear your heart
Racing,
Thinking,
Ticking over.

I smile into the window.
The air is crisp.
You breathe out
Sighs
And your eyes are pools of blue.

Let me take this moment
To love you
Because we may not have it
Ever again.

Four

I think it's really important to know your own soul.
That way, when the time comes, and you get old,
And your Mrs or fella gone done popped their clogs,
You can keep going, not fed to the dogs.

It's really important to go for a walk
And with yourself, have a little talk.
Ask yourself how you are, how the day's been,
But don't get too forward. No need to look keen!

Friends, mates, pals - I've had them by the bucket.
Inject me with venom and they'd probably suck it.
Tell them I'm hurting, they'd be on the phone,
But I still think it's important to spend time alone.

I've hugged myself while nobody's looking.
Venom alert? I've done the sucking
Of these my own bones, to preserve my own state.
If you learn nothing else, learn to be your best mate.

Johanna

You're the buzz beneath these '60s slats,
The echo of telly as you're cooking the fats,
The radio chat as you're humming the tune,
The last one who's stirring as time reaches noon.

Faint coughs I have heard, the occasional laugh,
The ring of your phone, the empty carafe.
Your soul is far-reaching, your smile is full.
Without you I'm sure that this house would be dull.

Lately I've felt that I'm reigning me in.
I'm stopping myself just to let you begin.
And so, dear warm soul, I have to be off.
This place was a home but I'll be better off-

In a home of my own. So do not miss
The creak of the floorboards, the faint, tender bliss
That comes with knowing tired souls like mine.
Maybe we'll meet in a simpler time.

Ducks

Your eyes are like
Two great spheres
And they see into my
Wounded soul.

I've lost the emptiness
Which created me
And as we sit on that garden bench,
I feel your hand gravitate toward my own.

I resist
And I kick up stones
And I scowl at the ducks
Who quack as though things are alright.

You nibble on my cheek,
You create a fun pastime.
From the corner of my mouth
Is the impish hint of a smile.

Tide

Part of you wants to go,
The other wishes to stay.
You crave the beaches of purple sands
And the laying on of unknown hands.
The tide comes in and takes your troubles away.

Enough of you has dreamt of this,
The other is a realist!
You keep a diary of jobs to do.
The bus pulls up, collects the Granny, plus you.
The rain is something you won't miss.

You've searched for apartments, flights, costs,
Thought of the way that you might tell your boss.
Your laundry is done, pressed, hung up,
Heating on, telly, dinner well-cooked,
As you sit with your mind, overtiming and lots.

No part of you wishes to go.
All of you wishes to stay.

You crave the curls of familiar lands,
The tender touch of well-known hands.
The tide is out, girl. Go and play.